Beer on th

The Craft Brew...

Volume Three:

Southeast Alaska

By Bill Howell

Photos by Elaine Howell

Foreword by Tom Dalldorf

Respect the cold. Alaska is a vast, rugged, beautiful but unforgiving region known for wilderness, fish and game and adventure in the warmer months and somewhat more challenging activities in winter. I have been coming to Anchorage in the dead of winter every year for some 20 years to experience the fruit of the brewer's art visiting breweries, attending beer dinners and judging at the now famous Great Alaskan Beer & Barley Wine festival.

Brewing in Alaska combines the struggle of creating artfully crafted beverages from resources mostly imported from the "lower 48" with the added complication of extreme weather and unpredictable supply lines. Traveling the state in the summer months, given the distances involved and road conditions, can be daunting but almost impossible in the frozen darkness of winter. Several small breweries around the state simply hibernate in winter and are reborn in the spring. For the traveling beer enthusiast, this can be an expensive and time-consuming task indeed.

Bill Howell is a retired Navy man with a passion

for beer. An avid homebrewer, Bill experienced the beer culture of England and Europe during his Navy years. This, combined with his thirst for beer history and literature, resulted in his creating a beer appreciation course "The Art and History of Brewing," that he teaches annually at the University of Alaska.

Bill's latest book, "Beer on the Last Frontier: The Craft Breweries of Alaska," is the result of his years of exploring the state's extended and extensive beer scene. From the early days to the more established breweries, here is a chance to get a sense of what creating great beer in a beautiful if rugged and challenging environment can be like.

I was privileged to witness some of the early years of brewing including Bird Creek Brewery. This small and ruggedly individualistic brewery was created by the iconoclastic Ike Kelly who built most of his own brewing equipment, did the brewing, and then played music at night on his makeshift stage to the delight of his thirsty fans. His classic *Old 55 Pale Ale* continues to this day thanks to the brewers at Silver Gulch Brewing in Fairbanks.

Alaskan Brewing began as a tiny operation in land-locked Juneau, the state's capitol, where every resource is either flown in or barged in. Owners and founders Geoff and Marcy Larsen took a note from the German brewers of Franconia and started to smoke the malt for their porter in a smokehouse adjacent to the brewery used mostly for smoking salmon. This stunning beer continues as one of the most medal-winning beers ever at the Great American Beer Festival. Alaska Brewing continues as the largest brewery in the state.

Yet another young couple, Mark Staples and Barb Miller, put their hopes and dreams into a small brewing operation in an industrial area of Anchorage some 20 years ago and now produce some of the best and most innovative beers in the state and on a much grander scale.

Alaska is a destination for most of us and now the adventure-seeking beer lover has this wonderful and informative backgrounder to guide the way and give context to a great Alaska beer adventure. And please, respect the cold.

Tom Dalldorf, editor and publisher, Celebrator Beer News

Table of Contents

Introduction

As anyone who has ever been here can tell you, Alaska is a special place. Sometimes it's special in a good way, sometimes it's special in a bad way, but it's never ordinary. Here in The Great Land, we live a lot closer to the edge than most people do Outside (what Alaskans call the rest of the world). Those folks can tell themselves that Nature has been tamed by Man; we Alaskans know better.

Looking out the authors' living room window on 6/20/2011

It takes a certain kind of person to choose to live in a place as remote and rugged as Alaska. Some people are born to it, but choose to leave as soon as they can. Often they return after a year or two, finding nowhere else in the world holds the allure of the Far North. Others come up for a visit or a vacation or a job and never leave. Be Warned: If Alaska grabs hold of you, no other place in the whole wide world will ever seem like home again.

Alaska is unique in its climate, its wildlife and the people who live here. Is it any surprise that our beers are unique as well? Beers, wines, meads, distilled spirits: they are all made commercially here in Alaska. And not just made, but made well. Alaska's alcoholic beverages are the frequent winners of awards in national and even international competitions. There are 25 commercial breweries in Alaska, three wineries, a meadery, and five distilleries. Not bad for a state with under 800,000 total residents.

This book series is an exploration and guide to the craft breweries making exceptional beers for Alaskans to drink. This volume covers Southeast Alaska, also known as the Panhandle, thanks to its shape. Volume I, published in 2012, covered the Kenai Peninsula and Kodiak Island. Volume II, published in 2103, covered Anchorage, Fairbanks, and all points in between. It is not intended to be a stand-alone guide to the parts of Alaska it covers. Rather, it should be viewed as a supplement, one which will point the visitor who is particularly interested in experiencing craft beer in Alaska in the right direction.

Juneau

The capital of Alaska, Juneau, is unique in that it can only be reached by ferry or by air; there are no roads connecting it to the rest of the state. Confined to a narrow strip on land between the Gastineau Channel and Mount Juneau, it is considered by many to be the most picturesque of all the state capitals in the United

States. Despite its isolation, Juneau hosts hundreds of thousands of tourists each year, thanks to the numerous cruise ships that ply the scenic Inside Passage. The 1880 discovery of gold in Gold Creek at the center of modern-day Juneau by prospectors Richard Harris and Joe Juneau lead to the founding of the town. Since then, more gold has been mined from this area than anywhere else in the world, but modern-day Juneau's primary industries are state government and tourism.

The city's downtown area, within easy walking distance of the cruise ship docks, is home to several historic saloons. Besides its interesting history, Juneau is also home to the oldest and by far the largest craft brewery in Alaska, the **Alaskan Brewing Company**. Founded in 1986, this brewery is one of the twenty largest craft breweries in the country.

Sitka

As with much of Southeast Alaska, Sitka is steeped in history. Designated in 1808 as the capital of Russian Alaska, it was the location for the formal transfer of sovereignty to the United States on October 18, 1867. It served as capital of the American Territory of Alaska until supplanted by Juneau in 1906.

Today, Sitka's primary industries are commercial fishing and tourism. Located on the western side of Baranof Island, it is accessible only by air or ferry and is home to the **Baranof Island Brewing Company**.

Haines & Skagway

Located at the northernmost end of the Inside Passage, Haines and Skagway are 20 miles apart by water but 250 miles apart by road. Skagway is home to the Klondike Gold Rush National Historical Park and, like Juneau, receives hundreds of thousands of cruise ship visitors each summer, all eager to explore its boardwalks and gift shops. Haines is a terminus for the Alaska-Canada highway; vehicles coming by ferry up the Inside Passage unload here and drive to the rest of Alaska. It also hosts a world-famous Bald Eagle Festival each November.

Both Skagway and Haines are home to breweries. The **Skagway Brewing Company** is a brewpub & restaurant, bearing a proud name that dates all the way back to 1898 and the Klondike Gold Rush. Skagway is also the home to **Gold Rush Brewing Company**. The **Haines Brewing Company** is a craft brewery with an extremely loyal local following and a statewide reputation for brewing exceptional beers. Haines is also the location of the oldest craft beer festival in Alaska; the **Great Alaska Craft Beer and Homebrew Festival** is held in each May on the State Fairgrounds there.

The Alaska-Canada Highway

One of the greatest road trips in North America is to drive the Alaska-Canada Highway, also known as the Al-Can, or simply the Alaska Highway. Starting in Dawson Creek, British Columbia, this road travels 1,387 miles through some of the most magnificent scenery on the planet, before ending in Delta Junction, Alaska. Carved out of a wilderness in the early days of

World War II under some of the harshest conditions imaginable, it represents a truly amazing engineering achievement. Even today, driving it gives one a real sense of adventure.

For the craft beer lover, however, it can be a pretty tough road. You'll pass your last craft brewery long before you reach Dawson Creek (either in Prince George, BC, if approaching from the south or Edmonton, AB, if coming from the east), and with only one exception, there won't be any more until you reach the promised land of Alaska. The only oasis in this long desert of craft beer is Whitehorse, the capital of the Yukon Territory, which is home to both the **Yukon Brewing Company** and the **Winterlong Brewing Company**. The former is a long-established regional craft brewery, while the latter is a nanobrewery that opened in the spring of 2015. An annual beer festival is also held each October in Whitehorse.

From Whitehorse, instead of pushing straight on through to Alaska, you might consider diverting south to visit Skagway, then taking the short ferry ride to Haines, and driving north on the Haines Highway to rejoining the Al-Can Highway at Haines Junction. Or you might go north from Whitehorse to visit the historic gold town of Dawson, the goal of the Klondike Stampeders in 1898, before continuing on to Alaska.

Map

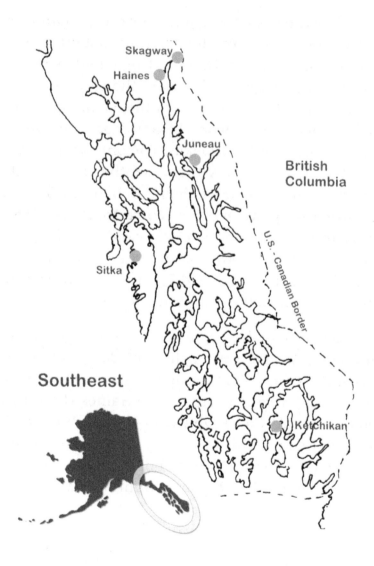

Skagway

Haines

Juneau

British
Columbia

U.S. - Canadian Border

Sitka

Southeast

Ketchikan

Alaskan Brewing Company

Location:

5429 Shaune Dr.

Juneau, Alaska 99801-9540

Phone: 907-780-5866

Email: info@alaskanbeer.com

Website: http://www.alaskanbeer.com/

Hours of Operation:

      May - September: 11 a.m. - 7 p.m., 7 days a week.

Driving Directions: Drive north out of downtown Juneau on Egan Drive/AK-7 for 4.5 miles. Turn right onto Vanderbilt Hill Road, which will become Glacier Highway after half a mile. Continue for another half mile, and then take a right onto Anka St. Take the second right onto Shaune Dr. The brewery is a large complex on the left.

Alaskan Brewing also owns a retail store in the historic Simpson Building of downtown Juneau.

Overview

Today, the Alaskan Brewing Company stands like a colossus over the craft brewing scene in Alaska. The little company that Geoff and Marcy Larson started in 1986 has grown into one of the largest and most respected manufacturing businesses in the state and the 20th largest craft brewer in the US (2014). Its beers have brought home more than 100 major medals and awards, almost half of which are gold, and the brewery has received a dozen awards as a business. Despite its phenomenal growth and tremendous economic successes, Alaskan Brewing has managed to sustain a strong commitment to both the local community and the natural environment in which it functions.

Marcy & Geoff Larson, the founders of Alaskan Brewing

Brewery Characteristics

As you'd expect for a brewery its size, beer production at Alaskan is a major operation. The brewery uses a 100-barrel brewhouse to produce its regular releases. However, Alaskan has retained its original 10-barrel brewhouse, which was first used back in 1986 when the brewery opened. Today, this brewhouse serves as Alaskan's pilot brewery, allowing the production of experimental brews for its Rough Draft Series (see below). To support its production, Alaskan also has a bottling line and a canning line.

100-barrel production brewhouse at Alaskan

One unique aspect of Alaskan Brewing is its heavy emphasis on sustainability. As it is located on an island, from its earliest days the brewery has been concerned about its environmental footprint and its impact on the quality of life for its neighbors. Consequently, Alaskan has always been an early adopter of new technologies which increased its sustainability and reduced its impact. After a major expansion in the mid-1990s, Alaskan was forced to begin shipping its spent grain south to Olympia, WA, as the small number of Juneau farmers could no longer use it all. To reduce the weight and increase the stability of this grain, Alaska became the first craft brewery in the country to install a grain dryer. In 1998, Alaskan also became the first craft brewery to begin capturing and recycling the CO_2 produced by fermentation. In 2008, Alaskan replaced its lauter tun with a mash press, allowing it to significantly increase the extraction from its brewing grain, while using less water. In 2012, the brewery made national headlines by installing a boiler that was fired exclusively by the dried, spent grain, cutting the brewery's energy costs by 70%.

The Brewer Speaks

Rob Day, Brewing Manager, in his own words:

How did you become a commercial brewer?

"I was a home brewer and loved to make beer. Being able to do something I enjoyed made it an easy decision to brew commercially."

What do you see as the biggest challenges facing a craft brewer in Alaska?

"There are several challenges facing a brewer in Alaska. The main one in Juneau is finding and getting fresh ingredients for our beer. The other one is getting our beer out to the wide variety of communities we have in Alaska. The cost of shipping raw materials in and finished product out is a constant challenge for us because we need to keep our prices competitive, and that is difficult the farther away from Juneau that we are selling our beer."

Alaskan's mash press, which replaces the lauter tun

What characteristics do you think define Alaskan craft beer, as opposed to craft beer brewed elsewhere?

"We have to be creative not only with our beer but with how we brew our beer and run our plant. It's not easy getting materials shipped in and out of Alaska. We are also sensitive about our waste, which is a big part of the reason we have set up our Spent Grain boiler, to use that waste product as a fuel source. We have always looked for ways to be more efficient and at the same time protect the community and environment where we live. In 1998 we were the first craft brewery in the US to install a CO_2 recovery system, and now we have a closed loop on CO_2 and same hundreds of thousands of pounds of carbon we would otherwise have to off-gas into the atmosphere. That kind of innovation helps define how we brew craft beer in Alaska."

Where do you think Alaskan craft brewing in general and your brewery/brewpub in particular will be in eight to ten years?

"There will be more breweries opening up in Alaska, and I think we will start to get more noticed for the beers produced in Alaska. We continue to have an overall goal of healthy and sustainable growth for Alaskan Brewing. But my main goals for our brewery in 10 years would be to still produce great beer and still have fun doing it."

The Beers

Alaskan Brewing Company divides it beers into four categories: Year Round, Seasonal, Limited Edition, and Rough Drafts. We will look at each in turn.

Year Round Beers

Amber Ale: This is the first beer released by Alaskan Brewing Company in 1986. It is based on a beer brewed by the Douglas City Brewery just outside Juneau in the early 1900s. Stylistically, it is a German altbier, with emphasis on rich malt flavor rather than hops. It has received numerous awards, including gold medals at the Great American Beer Festival and being voted "Best Beer in the Nation" in the 1988 GABF Consumers Poll. 5.3% ABV, 18 IBUs. It is available on draft, bottles, and cans almost everywhere in Alaska.

White Ale: This is the brewery's interpretation of the popular Belgian-style witbier. Spiced with the traditional coriander and orange peel, this beer is light and effervescent, with a smooth body. 5.3% ABV, 15 IBUS. It is available on draft and in bottles.

The boiler fired by spent grain

Stout: This oatmeal stout was originally part of the Rough Draft series, but its popularity led to it being added to Alaskan's year-round offerings in 1998. The addition of oats to the mash produces a balanced, smooth beer with notes of coffee and caramel. 5.7% ABV, 28 IBUs. Available on draft and in bottles.

Dried, spent grain at Alaskan

Icy Bay IPA: Alaskan Brewing was relatively late in adding an IPA to its stable of brews, releasing its first, under the name *Alaskan IPA*, in 2007. In 2014, the brewery changed the name of the beer to *Icy Bay IPA* and changed its hop profile, adding Bravo and Calypso to the Cascade, Summit and Apollo hops used in the original recipe. This IPA is not as aggressively hopped as most West Coast IPAs, remaining closer to the style's English roots. 6.2% ABV, 65 IBUs. Available on draft, in bottles, and in cans.

Freeride APA: Another beer which got its start in the Rough Draft series, *Freeride APA* was released as a year-round beer in early 2013. This beer replaced the venerable *Alaskan Pale Ale*, which the brewery discontinued later that year. Brewed with Cascade, Citra, and Centennial hops, this beer scores high in both flavor and drinkability. 5.3% ABV, 40 IBUs. Available on draft, in bottles, and in cans.

Hopothermia Double IPA: While it was late to the IPA arms race, Alaskan has been making up for lost time with releases such as this one. *Hopothermia DIPA* graduated from the Rough Draft series to year-round release in early 2014. Nugget and Apollo hops added in the brew kettle provide a green, floral aroma and citrus hop base, while the later addition of Amarillo, Citra, and Centennial hops add notes of spicy grapefruit and orange – complimenting the resilient malt profile. 8.5% ABV, 70 IBUs. Available in bottles and on draft.

Alaskan Brewing's taproom

Imperial Red Ale: The latest addition to Alaskan's year-round offerings, a full-bodied deep mahogany ale with ruby red highlights. A blend of

Bravo, El Dorado, Meridian and Summit hops give it an array of flavors ranging from pineapple and cherry to green mint and hibiscus, on top of the nutty, roasted caramel and subtle dried fruit flavors of the complex malt profile. 8.5% ABV, 80 IBUs. Available on draft and in bottles.

Seasonal Beers

Note: While its *Summer* and *Winter Ales* are perennial offerings, Alaskan Brewing frequently changes its spring and summer seasonal from year to year.

Summer Ale: Brewed in the Kolsch style, this light, golden ale balances a softly malted palate with the clean freshness of hops.5.3% ABV, 18 IBUs. Available in bottles and on draft.

Winter Ale: Brewed in the style of an English Old Ale, this ale balances the sweet heady aroma of Sitka spruce tips with the clean crisp finish of noble hops. Brewing with spruce tips has a long and distinguished history in Alaska, dating back to the exploratory voyages of Captain James Cook. 6.2% ABV, 22 IBUs. Available in bottles and on draft.

Big Mountain Pale Ale: The Spring 2015 seasonal, this American Pale Ale pours a clear and light copper in color. It has three domestic malt varieties providing firm footing for the distinct flavor and aroma of dry-hopped Simcoe and Mosaic. Notes of Asian pear, pine, and lemon in the aroma are answered by the toasted nut, biscuit and toffee malt. The crisp flavor is distinct from the aroma, with pleasantly strong herbal notes and hints of complex tropical fruit. 5.7% ABV, 45 IBUs. Available in bottles and on draft.

Pumpkin Porter: With over 11 pounds of pumpkin added to every barrel of this imperial porter, this beer has a smooth, velvety rich texture. Brown sugar, holiday spices and a touch of Alaskan's famous alder-smoked malt are added to create an aroma and flavor reminiscent of grandma's Thanksgiving pumpkin pie. 7.0% ABV, 25 IBUs. Available in bottle and on draft.

Limited Edition Beers

Alaskan Smoked Porter: Originally released in 1988, this famous beer was the first modern American smoked beer. Brewed using malt smoked over alder wood, this beer is released on November 1st each year in vintage dated, bottle-conditioned 22 oz. bombers. It has proved exceptionally suitable for cellaring, with bottles remaining in excellent condition for over two decades. It has dark, robust body and pronounced smoky flavor, which gradually changes over the years. 6.5% ABV, 45 IBUs. Available in bottles and on draft.

Pilot Series: This is a rotating series of beers, released on draft and in 20 oz. bottles. In the years where it is produced Alaskan's *Barley Wine Ale* appears as part of this series. Other entries have included *Imperial Rye Ale, Baltic Porter, Double Black IPA,* and *Raspberry Wheat Ale.*

Distribution and Availability

Alaskan Brewing Company's beers are distributed widely across Alaska and in Arizona, California, Colorado, Idaho, Michigan, Minnesota, Montana, Nevada, New Mexico, North Dakota, Oregon, South Dakota, Texas, Washington, Wisconsin and Wyoming. Its Rough Draft series are usually available only in select Alaskan and Pacific Northwest venues.

Baranof Island Brewing Company

Location:

215 Smith St.

Sitka, AK 99835

Phone: 907-747-2739

Email: info@baranofislandbrewing.com

Website: baranofislandbrewing.com

Hours of Operation:

12 PM to 8 PM, daily.

Driving Directions: From downtown Sitka, head east on Sawmill Creek Road, along the northern boundary of the Sitka National Historic Park. Take a left on Smith St.; the brewery will be on your left.

Overview

Baranof Island Brewing Company was founded in the historic town of Sitka by the husband and wife team of Rick and Suzan Armstrong in 2010. Their experience was similar to that of many small brewery start-ups in Alaska: the small system they initially purchased was soon overwhelmed by the tremendous local demand for their beer. After purchasing a larger system, Baranof Island began to look at packaging and distribution. On February 11, 2014, Baranof Island Brewing Company was granted a $350,000 development loan by the Mayor and City Assembly of Sitka. The loan was granted from The Southeast Alaska Economic Development Revolving Loan, also known as the Stevens Fund. It allowed the brewery to purchase a new grain mill, more fermentation tanks, and a canning line.

Conical fermenters at Baranof Island Brewing Company

Brewery Characteristics

Baranof Island Brewing Company began its existence with a miniscule 0.5-barrel system. As is typical for most brewery start-ups in Alaska, local demand quickly outstripped production capacity. In response, the brewery upgraded to a 1.75-barrel system. This larger system also soon proved inadequate, and Baranof Island is now using a 10-barrel brewhouse, a specially constructed system which is direct-fired via propane. Initially, the brewery used open fermentation, but has since shifted to closed fermenters. Besides offering its beers on draft, the brewery also offers several of its beers in 22 oz. bottles, and its *Silver Bay IPA* in cans.

The Brewer Speaks

Brewer Mike DesRosiers and Owner Rick Armstrong

31

Owner Rick Armstrong in his own words:

How did you become a commercial brewer?

"It started in the 90's while attending the University of Montana. The craft beer scene was exploding and always intrigued me. From there, it was just a matter of connecting the dots to the right people that would help me make it all happen."

What do you see as the biggest challenges facing a craft brewer in Alaska?

"Just the pure size and remoteness of Alaska brings big challenges. Shipping costs are outrageous, the population base is spread out and there are no roads in or out for the most part."

What characteristics do you think define Alaskan craft beer, as opposed to craft beer brewed elsewhere?

"Alaska may be the largest state; however our community of brewers is very close. When the different breweries get together we all know each other and we all get along very well which makes it a very cool thing as we all help each other."

Where do you think Alaskan craft brewing in general and your brewery/brewpub in particular will be in eight to ten years?

"We plan to grow right along with the industry and believe it will continue to grow for quite some time. Our new canning line is customer driven so we are excited to see where else our customers take us! In the last six months we have almost tripled our brewing capacity and we are always planning for the next addition whatever that might be from bigger fermenters to more seating."

The interior of Baranof Island Brewing Company

The Beers

Regular Beers:

Peril Strait Pale Ale: Brewed from 2-row, crystal, and wheat malts and hopped with Nugget, Cascade, and Willamette hops, this is a classic American Pale Ale. It pairs well with many foods, especially local shellfish. 5.5% ABV, 26 IBUs. Available on draft and in 22 oz. bottles.

Medvejie Stout: Derived from the Russian word for bear, and also the name of a local lake, *medvejie* is pronounced meh-du-VEE-gee locally. This is a strong American Stout, made using flaked oats, roasted barley, and chocolate malts, and then hopped with Nugget, Cascade, and Willamette. 7.25% ABV, 43 IBUs. Available on draft and in 22 oz. bottles.

Silver Bay IPA: This American IPA is brewed from 2-row, crystal, wheat, and carapils, and hopped with Nugget, Cascade, and CTZ hops. 6.5% ABV, 54 IBUs. It is available on draft, in 22 oz. bottles, and in cans.

Redoubt Red Ale: Brewed using only 2-row and crystal, this red ale's complexity belies its simple malt bill, thanks to a hop schedule that includes Nugget, Cascade, CTZ, and Mt. Hood hops. 5.75% ABV, 40 IBUs. Available on draft and in 22 oz. bottles.

Baranof Brown Ale: Sweeter than the typical American Brown Ale, this beer has an extensive malt bill, including 2-row, crystal, brown, chocolate, and black malt, along with roasted barley and flaked oats. It is lightly hopped with Nugget, Cascade, and CTZ hops. 6.25% ABV, 19 IBUs. Available on draft or in 22 oz. bottles.

A sampler of Baranof Island's beers

Seasonal Beers

Sitka Spruce Tip Ale: You can't get much more iconic that spruce tip ale in Alaska, and Baranof Island produces this beer each spring. It pours a clear ruby with a nice cream-colored head. The aroma is of sweet malt and the piney spruce tips. Carbonation is good, as is its mouthfeel. The flavor profile has a good malt backbone, balanced by the piney, resiny spruce notes. Hops are unobtrusive. A real "taste of Alaska" beer. 6.5% ABV. Available on draft or in 22 oz. bottles each spring.

Halibut Point Hefeweizen: A nice German-style Hefeweizen, brewed with actual Bavarian yeast. Look for banana, clove, and bubblegum notes in the aroma. Brewed primarily from wheat malt, with the addition of 2-row, Vienna, and crystal malts, and lightly hopped with Nugget, Cascade, and CTZ hops. 5.0% ABV, 16

IBUs. Available on draft and in 22 Oz. bottles each summer.

Two-head manual canning machine

Distribution and Availability

Baranof Island Brewing Company's beers are distributed throughout Alaska by the Odom Corporation.

Gold Rush Brewing Company

Location:

Mile 2 Klondike Hwy

Skagway, AK 99840

Phone: (907) 983-2434

Email: info@goldrushbrewery.com

Website: http://goldrushbrewery.com/

Hours of Operation:

Note: This brewery is open only during the summer season, May to September, during which it is open seven days a week. Check its website or call for the exact hours.

Driving Directions: From the Skagway ferry terminal, head north out of town on Klondike Highway (AK-98). The brewery will be on your right at Mile Marker 2.

Overview

The Gold Rush Brewing Company is part of the Klondike Gold Fields, a tourist attraction a couple of miles north of the historic town of Skagway, on the Klondike Highway, which connects that town to the city of Whitehorse and the Al-Can Highway. Since it is primarily aimed at the busy summer tourist season, when thousands of visitors arrive each day via cruise ships, the entire facility is only open from May through September. The Klondike Gold Fields has been open since May of 2000, and the brewery was added in 2009. In early 2015, the brewery underwent a significant expansion, including the purchase of a new and larger brewhouse.

The original Gold Rush brewhouse, before going all-grain in 2015.

Brewery Characteristics

Until it expansion in 2015, the beers which could be produced by Gold Rush Brewing were restricted due to the limitations of its brewing equipment. Lacking a true mash tun, the brewery was forced to use hopped extract to produce its beers, though it was possible to do partial mash brewing for certain special beers. Recognizing these constraints this placed on the brewery and its beers, in the winter of 2014 a new 10-bbl brew kettle and mash tun were purchased. The brewery took delivery in May of 2015 and has been producing all-grain beers since then.

The Brewer Speaks

Robert Butker, Gold Rush Brewer

Brewer Robert Butker in his own words:

How did you become a commercial brewer?

"In the fall of 2011, Mike Vondette, one of the owners at Gold Rush, happened to be visiting Atlanta,

Georgia where I was living at the time. He and I had a mutual friend, Eric, who I invited over to brew. It was a pumpkin brown ale for the record. Two weeks later, Mike offered me a job up here. I took it and I have not regretted it since."

What do you see as the biggest challenges facing a craft brewer in Alaska?

"Logistics. Especially up here in the Northern Lynn Canal, it is very often difficult for us to source high quality ingredients at reasonable prices that will be delivered properly and in a timely fashion."

What characteristics do you think define Alaska craft beer, as opposed to craft beer brewed elsewhere?

"One of the biggest advantages to brewing up here is the water. Down south every batch of beer I ever did, I would have to filter the water treat the water or by the water. In Skagway, that is unnecessary."

Where do you think Alaska craft brewing in general and your brewery/brewpub in particular will be in eight to ten years?

"Alaskan craft brewing has nowhere to go but up in our opinion. As Alaska becomes a more and more popular destination for tourism while American craft beer is currently undergoing a boom/renaissance, I see bright things in our future."

The Beers

Regular Beers:

Fireweed Honey Wheat Ale: Pours a light gold color with a white head that left good lacing on the glass. The nose has notes of sweet honey and banana, which you also find in the taste. There is a long, sweet banana finish. 7.2% ABV. Available on draft and in bottles.

Treeline IPA: This beer is closer to an English-style IPA, rather than an American-style, meaning that it is not as aggressively hopped as a West Coast IPA. It has a medium body with a pleasantly hoppy aroma with balancing malt backbone. 5% ABV, 50 IBUs.

Blue Collar Brew: This brew was created as an ode to the lost American Golden Ales, a highly popular pre-prohibition beer style that was one of the most popular throughout the American west. Pours a golden color, with a white head. Good carbonation, with a light mouthfeel. Slightly sweet on the palate, similar in style to a cream ale. 5.0 % ABV. Available on draft and in bottles.

Seasonal Beers:

Adventure Series: This is the name Gold Rush gives to its specialty brews, such as *Dark Days Imperial Stout* and *RX Chill Pils*. Check the menu to see what is on offer when you visit.

Distribution and Availability

Since Gold Rush Brewing Company is licensed as a brewpub, Alaska law prohibits it from distributing its beers offsite. Beers are typically available by the glass, by the growler, or in bottles.

Haines Brewing Company

Location:

Southeast Alaska State Fairgrounds

108 White Fang Way

Haines, AK 99827

Phone: 907-766-3823

Email: hainesbrew@gmail.com

Website: www.hainesbrewing.com

Special Note: Haines Brewing Company is currently constructing a new brewery. It will be located at the corner of 4th and Main St. in downtown Haines. It is scheduled to open in September, 2015.

Hours of Operation:

1pm - 6pm : Monday-Saturday and expanding hours at its new location.

Driving Directions: From the Haines Highway (AK -7) turn south onto Fair Road. The brewery is located in Dalton City on the State Fairgrounds.

Overview

One of the older craft breweries in Alaska, Haines Brewing Company was established in 1999 by avid homebrewer Paul Wheeler and his wife Jeanne Kitayama. Starting off brewing in used dairy tanks, demand for this brewery's beers quickly forced a shift to closed fermenters. None of the brewery's beers are filtered or pasteurized, and so they are typically only available locally. As mentioned above, Haines Brewing is currently located in extremely cramped quarters on the Southeast Alaska State Fairgrounds, but construction is underway on a new brewery in downtown Haines.

Brewery Characteristics

Currently, Haines Brewing Company is using a 3.5-barrel brewhouse in its cramped location, along with several conical fermenters. The brewery is so small, it lacks a true taproom, having only room enough for a serving counter, just inside its door. Patrons are typically forced to take their beers outside to consume them, which is hardly ideal, given the rainy climate of Southeast Alaska.

Haines Brewing's cramped quarters

When its new brewery is completed in September of 2015, Haines Brewing will have a new 7-barrel brewhouse, more fermentation tanks, and a true 750-square foot taproom, which should allow its patrons to enjoy their beer indoors.

The view from Haines Brewing's service counter.

The Brewer Speaks

Paul Wheeler, Haines Brewing Co.

Owner/Brewer Paul Wheeler in his own words:

How did you become a commercial brewer?

"Like many others, I started out as a homebrewer, because there was no such thing as a real beer when I arrived in Haines in the 1980's. By 1999 I saw the niche for locally-brewed beer, and so with the encouragement of friends we started the Haines Brewing Company."

What do you see as the biggest challenges facing a craft brewer in Alaska?

"The cost of shipping is such a big expense, with heavy ingredients and heavy products. Also, geographically we are so spread out across the state that it's difficult for brewers to collaborate."

What characteristics do you think define Alaska craft beer, as opposed to craft beer brewed elsewhere?

"There's no difference. Like craft brewers everywhere we have a passion to produce a quality beer crafted in our own communities. I don't think we can define Alaska brewers just because we are up north; we're no different than brewers anywhere else in the world."

Where do you think Alaska craft brewing in general and your brewery/brewpub in particular will be in eight to ten years?

"I think it's exciting to see the growth in Alaska still continuing with new breweries starting up in each community. There's always room for more and innovative brewing, just as we see it happening elsewhere, and see that people are willing to risk entering into the industry. It's also exciting to see the craft beer drinkers expanding their experiences to support their local breweries."

"Haines Brewing Company will be on Main Street in Haines, same as it is but with a larger production capacity and more room for consumers to socialize. We will always be an integral part of our community of Haines. We are the local brewery in our community, and we don't strive to be a regional brewery. We don't need to be on shelves in the Lower 48, or all across Alaska for that matter. We have no intention of trying to duplicate or compete in that market. So in 10 years, we'll still be the local brewery."

The Beers

Regular Beers:

Black Fang Imperial Stout: Pours richly dark with a nice tan head that leaves excellent lacing on the glass. The aroma is decadent: dark chocolate, molasses, anise, and just a slight roasted/nutty smell. The flavor profile is similar, moving from a sweet start to a roasty, dry finish. Carbonation is good and the mouthfeel is medium, perhaps a bit lighter than is typical for this style of beer. 8.0% ABV.

Dalton Trail Pale Ale: Pours a clear gold with a nice white head. Aroma is of citrusy hops. Body is light and carbonation is good. Good bitterness, balanced by malt character. A highly drinkable English-style Pale Ale. 4.8% ABV

Devil Made Me Do It (DMMDI) IPA: Pours a golden-amber color with a nice head, with good lacing.

The aroma is both citric and piney from the East Kent Goldings hops used. There is a bit of a biscuity pale malt balance and just a little caramel smell. The flavor profile is similar to the aroma, with pine and grapefruit hop flavors providing the main elements. A slight hint of caramel and biscuit malt is noticeable, but the overriding character is hop goodness. 6.6% ABV

Lookout Stout: Pours a deep reddish black color, with a small off-white head. Nose is heavily toasted malts, with a roasted note that is quite nice. Flavor profile is more roasted malt notes, with a slight sweet milky quality. Very low hop flavor and bitterness allow the nice roasted grain flavor to shine through. 6.0% ABV.

Eldred Rock Red Ale: Pours an amber color with a tan head that left good lacing. The nose highlights the sweet and toasty malt notes, but there is also a hint of citrus from the hops. Nicely rounded, nutty malt flavors arrive on the palate first, followed by a sweet, light fruitiness. The fruitiness transitions from a mellow pear-like flavor to a hint of citrus hops, before a mineral-like, dry finish wipes the palate clean. 5.0% ABV

Seasonal and Specialty Beers:

Bigger Hammer Barley Wine: An English-style barley wine, this beer pours a dark ruby-brown color with a thin head. The aroma is of brown sugar and melted caramel. Carbonation is low, and it has a sticky mouthfeel. Flavor profile has sweet elements, like the nose, plus dark fruit as well. Aged versions exhibit sherry-like characteristics. Alcohol warmth is noticeable. 11.7% ABV.

Captain Cook's Spruce Tip Ale: Brewed on a brown ale base, this beer is Haines Brewing's interpretation of this ubiquitous Southeast Alaska style. It pours a hazy amber to orange color, with a white head that dissipates fairly quickly, but leaves nice lacing. The aroma contains a sweet spruce resinous quality and a slight sweet citrus note, which seem to combine nicely. The flavor is sweet but the combination of spruce and citrus fruit notes brings balance. The mouthfeel is slightly sharp but still carries a nice smooth sweetness across the tongue.

Distribution and Availability

Besides selling beer directly to the public at the brewery, Haines Brewing Company self-distributes its beers to many of the restaurants and bars in Haines. Unfortunately, its beers are seldom available anywhere else, though Haines does usually participate in the Great Alaska Beer & Barley Wine Festival, held each January in Anchorage. However, the best time to sample Haines Brewing's beers is at the Great Alaska Craft Beer and Homebrew Festival, held each Memorial Day weekend in Haines.

Skagway Brewing Company

Location:

7th Ave & Broadway

Skagway, Alaska 99840

Phone: 907-983-2739

Email: info@skagwaybrewing.com

Website: http://www.skagwaybrewing.com

Hours of Operation:

Bar opens at 10am Monday-Friday, 11am on Saturday and Sunday.

Lunch served 11am - 5pm. Dinner served 5pm - 10pm.

Nightly dine-in dinner specials begin at 6pm.

Driving Directions:

From the ferry terminal: Head north up Broadway; brewery will be on your right.

From the Klondike Highway (AK-98): Follow the highway into Skagway, where it becomes State Street. At 7th Avenue, take a left and go one block to Broadway.

Overview

The name Skagway Brewing Company is steeped in Alaskan brewing history. The first company to carry that name opened its doors in 1897 and brewed beer until 1905. The name lay fallow for almost a century, until it was resurrected in 1997 for a brewpub located in the Golden North Hotel, which operated until 2002. The brewery's equipment sat idle until 2007, when Mike Healy, a longtime Skagway resident, saw an opportunity and purchased both the derelict equipment and the brewery's name. He moved the brewery to a brand new building, located at 7th and Broadway, not far from where the original Skagway Brewing Company was located in 1898. On July 4, 2007, the Skagway Brewing Company again fired up its brew kettle and opened its doors, welcoming both locals and the thousands of tourists from the huge cruise ships which visit Skagway daily during the summer.

Interior of Skagway Brewing Company

Brewery Characteristics

The brewhouse at Skagway Brewing Company has all the hallmarks of a system that has been shoehorned into a space much too small. The brewhouse is a 4-barrel steam-fired system, manufactured by Elliot Bay Metal Fabricating Inc., and is crammed into a small, second story room, along with five conical fermenters. There are two 4-barrel fermenters, two 8 barrel fermenters, and one 12-barrel vessel. This limited production capacity supplies the eight brite tanks feeding the bar taps on the ground floor. Total annual production is approximately 300 barrels.

Skagway Brewing's cramped brewhouse

Recognizing the limitations of the current arrangement, Owner Mike Healy hopes to eventually construct a dedicated brewing facility nearby, which would allow all brewing to be moved off-site. This arrangement would allow Skagway Brewing to increase its annual production to the point where it could consider distributing its beers, either on draft or in bottles.

Restaurant Menu

Skagway Brewing Company serves a full menu for both lunch and dinner. There are the usual bar-type appetizers, such as home-made pretzels, French fries, and chicken wings, of course, but there is also a hearty selection of salads. There are numerous sandwiches on offer, including fried Alaskan halibut and grilled sockeye salmon, plus some seven specialty burgers. On the dinner menu, there is a steak of the day, plus several pasta dishes. Each night of the week there is a different nightly special, beginning at 6 pm.

The Brewer Speaks

Skagway Brewer Trevor Clifford and Owner Mike Healy

Brewer Trevor Clifford in his own words:

How did you become a commercial brewer?

"It all started with a Mr. Beer kit I got for Christmas in 2002. I hadn't ever thought of brewing before, but after picking up Palmer's brewing book and finding the nearest brew supply, I quickly set aside the kit and made my first batch from scratch. That led to five years of homebrewing in various closets, garages and basements. I also found that I enjoyed fabricating and tweaking my equipment as much as the brewing itself."

"In 2006 I met Mike through a mutual friend. He was a man with a plan, travelling the states in search of a brewer in order to re-establish Skagway's brewery which had been dormant for years. We chatted over a beer (Ninkasi, as this was in Eugene), and he offered me the job."

"I had lived in Anchorage (my wife's hometown) and was excited at the prospect of moving back to Alaska. I had even visited Skagway and noticed the old brewery equipment piled on a trailer on the side of the road (little did I know that I would be the one to revitalize it). So we took the plunge and made the move. I saw it as a lucky opportunity. Who knows, maybe I was simply the only one willing and able to take the chance on moving to Skagway in the winter to run a brewery that wasn't even built yet."

What do you see as the biggest challenges facing a craft brewer in Alaska?

"One of the biggest challenges is of course shipping logistics. With everything coming in by barge or plane and weather dependent, timing can be tough to have ingredients when you need them. You have to plan ahead and order early."

Brewer Trevor Clifford mashing in

"As with most Alaska breweries, our extreme seasonal population change is also quite the challenge. An influx of seasonal workers and thousands of tourists every day create a huge demand in the summer. Whereas in winter we're back to our 800 or so locals. This means going from near zero to absolute balls-out brewing while trying to accurately predict the next flux."

What characteristics do you think define Alaskan craft beer, as opposed to craft beer brewed elsewhere?

"I think sheer will power could be considered an ingredient in most Alaska beers. Our remoteness often means we have to improvise, make-do, and invent just to get things done. This of course can lead to beautiful things. I believe this sheer will power is truly reflected in the grain to glass aspect of brewing in Alaska. Also, our water is amazing."

Where do you think Alaskan craft brewing in general and your brewery/brewpub in particular will be in eight to ten years?

"There's no way to know what we don't know, but I think the craft beer culture has taken hold in Alaska and will continue to grow in one way or another. As for our brewery, we do have plans to expand. Before too long we'll have a new Brew Pub with greater capacity and a larger brewery to keep up with the demands of thirsty visitors."

The Beers

Regular Beers:

Prospector Pale Ale: This beer is a copper-colored American pale ale with a small white head. Initial citrus aromas compliment a soft bitterness that lingers into a smooth finish. Its flavor profile is clean and dry with a subtle hop character. 5.7% ABV

Chilkoot Trail IPA: Amarillo and Cascade are the hops of choice for this beer. Pours hazy amber with white head. Aroma is of citrusy hops, biscuit malt and ripe fruit. Body is medium and crisp. An assertive bitterness and soft alcohol warmth are supported by a strong malty backbone. Finish is long and orange-like.

Boom Town Brown Ale: This beer is brewed using nine different malts and harkens to the sweeter English version of this style, rather than the hoppier American interpretation. Pours brown with off-white head. Aroma is of bready, toasted malt, dark fruit, chocolate, coffee and cacao. Body is full and smooth. Taste is of bready, toasted malt, dark fruit, chocolate and coffee. Finish is long and dry. 5.6% ABV

Blue Top Porter: Pours dark brown with beige head. Aroma is of bready, toasted malt, dark fruit, chocolate, coffee and cacao. Body is fool and smooth. Taste is of bready, toasted malt, dark fruit, chocolate and coffee. Finish is long and dry.

Seasonal Beers:

Spruce Tip Blonde Ale: Skagway Brewing's version of this Southeast Alaska favorite. Pours a clear light orange-yellow color with a thin white head that dissipates steadily. Stringy lacing on the glass. Pine and spruce in the nose, along with some fresh fruit and spice. Medium-bodied with a nice woody character, and flavors of piney hops, malt and sweet fruit. The finish is fruity with the fresh spruce flavor lingering in the aftertaste. 5.5% ABV

Fresh spruce tips, the key ingredient for Spruce Tip Blonde Ale

Distribution and Availability

Since Skagway Brewing Company is licensed as a brewpub, its beers are only available on-site. Beers are typically available by the glass or by the growler. You might also encounter its brews at various beer festivals around the state.

Places to Find Craft Beer

Bars & Restaurants

The Bamboo Room & Pioneer Bar

13 2nd Avenue

907-766-3443
http://www.bamboopioneer.net/home

Opened in 1953, this place is a local legend. Breakfast, lunch, and dinner are served in The Bamboo Room, while the adjoining Pioneer Bar has a nice selection of Alaskan Brewing and Haines Brewing beers. Non-smoking.

Fireweed Restaurant

Historic Building #37

Blacksmith Road

907-766-3838   No website

One of the best restaurants in Haines, The Fireweed specializes in gourmet pizzas. Typically, there are four or five Haines Brewing beers on tap.

The Fogcutter Bar

188 Main St.

(907) 776-2555   http://haines.ak.us/fogcutter-bar

This is a great place to visit for a spot of local color, as opposed to the more touristy locations in Southeast. Ten beers on tap, including Haines Brewing and Alaskan Brewing brews. There are two pool tables, and a foosball table. Monday Night Football on big screen TVs. Dance floor. Open year round.

Mountain Market & Cafe

151 3rd Ave

907-766-3350   http://mountain-market.com/

This combination health food store, deli, and liquor store offers good food along with one of the best craft beer selections in town.

Festivals

Great Alaska Craft Beer and Homebrew Festival

Held each May at the State Fairgrounds in Haines, this festival is the oldest beer festival in Alaska, now in its 23rd year (2015). Held on Memorial Day weekend, it begins with a Gourmet Brewers' Dinner on Friday night in Harriet Hall on the fairgrounds. Each of the five courses of this dinner are accompanied by two beers from breweries attending the festival. It is so popular that the event typically sells out three months in advance. On Saturday afternoon, the beer festival itself is held on the fairgrounds, with numerous breweries and distributors from across Alaska and the Yukon Territory of Canada pouring their beers. While not the largest one in Alaska, this festival is very highly

regarded among both brewers and craft beer lovers.
http://www.seakfair.org/beer-fest/

Juneau

Bars & Restaurants

Alaskan Hotel and Bar

167 S. Franklin St.

(800) 327-9347   www.thealaskanhotel.com

This is the oldest operating hotel in Alaska, having first opened on Tuesday, September 16, 1913. The bar has frequent live performances and a good selection of local craft beers plus some Belgian imports.

The Hangar

2 Marine Way, #106

(907) 586-5018   www.hangaronthewharf.com

Located downtown right on the water, The Hangar offers an excellent selection of craft beers both on draft and in bottles, with 100+ brews on offer. The food is upscale pub grub, with an emphasis on fresh, local seafood.

The Imperial Billiard & Bar

241 Front St.

(907) 586-1960

This bar's claim to fame is that it is the oldest continuously operating bar in the state, so it's worth a visit from the historical standpoint. Otherwise, the bar is nothing special.

Package/Liquor Stores

Alaska Cache Liquors

156 S. Franklin St.

(907) 586-2232

Located downtown, this store has a reasonable selection of craft beers from around the state.

Festivals

Capital City Brewfest

Held each September downtown at the Juneau Arts and Cultural Center (JACC), this festival is a fundraiser for the Juneau Rotary.
http://www.capbrewfest.com/

Bars & Restaurants

With the notable exception of the Skagway Brewing Company, many of the town's bars and restaurants are only open during the summer tourist season, mid-April to mid-October. If you visit during the off-season, your choices will likely be very limited.

Red Onion Saloon

205 Broadway

(907) 983-2414   www.redonion1898.com

Formerly a bordello, this entirely authentic, restored establishment provides a glimpse into the Gold Rush era in Skagway. There is a tour of the bordello museum upstairs. There is a respectable offering of draft beers, mostly from Alaskan Brewing Company, as well as a decent list of bottled offerings. The food menu is typical bar fare, featuring pizza, sandwiches, and salads.

The Mascot Saloon

Corner Broadway and 3rd Ave

You won't be able to get a drink in this saloon, but it's well worth a visit nonetheless. Part of the Klondike Gold Rush National Park, this saloon is actually a museum. It has been restored to its appearance in late 1904. Open for the summer season, May to September.

Package/Liquor Stores

Alaska Liquor Store

264 2nd Ave

(907) 983-3888

Due to Skagway's small populations (approximately 850), this is the only liquor store in town. It has a fair selection of bottles and cans from craft breweries across the state.

Whitehorse, Yukon Territory

Breweries

While not technically part of the Alaska craft beer scene, there are two craft breweries now in operation in Whitehorse. If you are driving to Alaska via the Al-Can Highway, I highly recommend you allow yourself time to visit one or both of them.

Yukon Brewing Company
(www.yukonbeer.com)

Yukon Brewing is located in an industrial park on the north of town, at 102 Copper Road. It has been in business for fifteen years and has recently become a distillery as well, selling the hard stuff under the name

Yukon Spirits. To date it has released a botanical vodka and have whiskey aging in barrels, as well as plans for a chili-flavored gin. Yukon's beers are distributed into British Columbia and Alberta, as well as throughout the Yukon Territory.

The brewery itself is a substantial operation, with a 25-hectoliter brewhouse and 12 100-hectoliter conical tanks. (Converting from metric to something I understand, that's a 21.3-barrel brewhouse and 12 85.2-barrel tanks.) Yukon brews eight beers year-round and about fifteen specialty/seasonal beers over the course of a year. It bottles all eight year-round beers and also cans four of them, using an automated Cask Brewing canning system.

Perhaps the strangest aspect of this brewery is its use of recycled bottles. Given its remote location in Whitehorse, new bottles are quite expensive, costing 32 cents each. Instead, Yukon receives pallets of used bottles from the local recycling centers. Yukon sorts the bottles and sends back all clear or green ones, then runs all the amber bottles through a large cleaning machine that was built in the 1950s. Strong caustic dissolves everything organic (labels, cigarette butts, whatever), then the bottles are thoroughly rinsed and inspected, both by eye and laser for any cracks or chips. These clean bottles are then fed into the bottling line to be filled with Yukon beer. The end result is a savings of 27 cents per bottle, compared to buying them new.

During the summer, Yukon offers three tours a day, seven days a week, at noon, 2 PM, and 4 PM. Tours are capped at 10 people each, ensuring a small enough group for the guide to do a proper job. If your schedule is tight, they do take reservations, either the day of or the day prior to the tour you want. Call 867-668-4183 to book in advance. Tours cost $5 per person, all of which is donated to local charities.

The folks at Yukon Brewing do tours right. The one my wife and I took lasted about 90 minutes, rather than the advertised 30 to 40. The young lady guiding us around was eager to answer our questions, even the esoteric ones asked by yours truly. The tour concluded with a tasting of thirteen (!) different beers, which represented every beer that Yukon sells in cans or bottles, plus the five seasonal that were on tap at the brewery. Not bad for donating $5 to charity!

Its flagship brand is *Yukon Gold English Pale Ale*, available in bottles, cans, or on draft. This is the top-selling brand in the Yukon, outselling big Canadian brands like Molson and Labatt, and you will find it on draft everywhere. Its *Ice Fog IPA* is also available in both bottles and cans; it's in the style of an English rather than an American IPA, with an emphasis on floral English hops rather than IBUs. Yukon's strongest beer is *Lead Dog*, a dark Old Ale clocking in at 7% ABV. There's also *Midnight Sun Espresso Stout*, made using coffee from the local coffee roasters of the same name (not to be confused with beers from Midnight Sun Brewing in Anchorage).

The author ordering a beer in the taproom of Yukon Brewing Company

Winterlong Brewing Company
(www.winterlongbrewing.com)

This new brewery opened in Whitehorse in the spring of 2015. Winterlong Brewing Company is owned by Meghan & Marko Marjanovic. It received its license to brew on April 20, 2015, and opened to the public in May. A true nanobrewery, it is only open to the public

on Friday and Saturday afternoons. Check its website
for the latest schedule.

Festivals

Yukon Beer Festival

Held over two days each September at the
Kwanlin Dun Cultural Center in Whitehorse, this is a
relatively new but growing festival. Proceeds go to
support the Yukon Literacy Coalition. Besides the beers,
there are food vendors and live music.
http://yukonbeerfestival.com/

Looking Ahead

Southeast Alaska is a region rich in history, and included in that is a long history of brewing. As home to both the largest and some of the smallest of the breweries in the state, Southeast truly covers the full spectrum of brewing possibilities. Future developments in the craft beer scene in Southeast Alaska also look to be very promising.

The existing craft breweries show every sign of continuing growth. Alaskan Brewing has just completed a significant expansion and remains among the top 20 largest craft breweries in the nation. The planned completion of the new home for the Haines Brewing Company in downtown Haines should allow that excellent brewery to blossom after moving from its current cramped surrounding. Skagway Brewing has dreams of also building a new free-standing brewery, allowing it more room to grow. Gold Rush Brewing has just replaced its brewhouse, while Baranof Island continues to ramp up both production and distribution.

However, there is much more in the works. New breweries will likely be joining the list of existing ones very soon. The Baleen Brewing Company is working to opening in Ketchikan, which has lacked a brewery of its own since 1943. Tiny Gakona Brewing Company is close to firing up its Sabco Brew Magic System and making commercial brews in that tiny town in the Interior. Growler Bay hopes to open soon in the port city of

Valdez. It's truly an exciting time in the world of craft beer in Alaska!

With this volume, I conclude my survey of all the craft breweries in Alaska. My next project will be to revise and update Volumes One and Two, and then combine it with this one in a single edition. Look for the new, combined edition of **Beer on the Last Frontier: The Craft Breweries of Alaska** to be released in early 2016.

Until Next Time, Cheers!

About the Authors

One of the first questions I always ask about any guidebook is this: "What qualifies the author to give me advice on this particular subject or place?" So I think it's only fair that I answer that question by telling you a little bit about myself.

I've been a craft beer lover and homebrewer since 1989. From 1984 to 2004, I was an officer in the United States Navy, which allowed me to travel extensively and drink beers all over the world. From 1998 to 2001, I was fortunate enough to be stationed in London, and during those three years I travelled throughout Britain, as well as to Belgium, Germany, and the Czech Republic to sample the best beers each had to offer.

I retired from the Navy in 2004 and moved to Sterling on Alaska's Kenai Peninsula, taking a job at Kenai Peninsula College, which is part of the University of Alaska. As craft breweries and brewpubs began opening in the area, I convinced my college administration that it was time to offer a course on beer, and in the spring of 2007, I taught *The Art & History of Brewing* for the first time. It was a rousing success, and I have taught it again each year since.

Given the popularity of my course, starting a blog seemed the next logical step. My purpose in writing Drinking on the Last Frontier was mainly to keep my students, current and former, apprised of local beer developments. Much to my surprise, my blog developed quite a following, both within and outside of Alaska. Its popularity was such that I was offered a monthly beer column in one of our local papers, **The Redoubt Reporter**, in November 2009.

2/27/2010 at the Wynkoop Brewing Company in Denver

As I was riding the wave of this success, my wife convinced me to enter the **Wynkoop Brewing Company**'s Beerdrinker of the Year contest in December 2009. I didn't think I had much of a chance, but I was selected as one of the three finalists, and in the head-to-head competition in Denver on February 27, 2010, I actually won, much to my amazement. Deciding to accept this as a sign, my wife and I attended the Great American Beer Festival that year, something I hadn't done since 1990.

Since then, I have continued my efforts to educate folks about craft beer and to promote Alaska's craft breweries, both within and outside the 49th state. In 2012, I was hired by the **Northwest Brewing News** as their correspondent for Alaska, and I also began working on this book project. In addition to the **Beer on the Last Frontier** series, I am also the author of **Alaska Beer: Liquid Gold in the Land of the Midnight Sun**. That book is a history of brewing in Alaska, from the days of Russian rule to the present and was published in 2015 by The History Press.

You will certainly notice the many excellent photographs which illustrate this book. These are the work of my beautiful and talented wife, Elaine Howell, who graciously agreed to take part in this project by supplying those photographs.

The authors, Elaine and Bill Howell

This book is the third in a series of three volumes which describe the state of play of craft brewing in Alaska. As with any such guidebook, you may find that things have changed at a particular brewery since the time of writing; if so, please accept my apologies in advance. I intend to do my best to update this work on a regular basis, but the craft brewing scene in this state is a fast-moving target.

In spite of any such shortcomings, I hope you will find this work enlightening, entertaining, and useful. It represents a small gift back on my part to all the brewers who work hard every day to give us such exceptional beers to enjoy and to the citizens of the magnificent state of Alaska, which is now my home.

Made in the USA
Monee, IL
02 June 2022

97334208R00046